Elegy

Nick Payne's *If There Is I Haven't Found It Yet* was staged at the Bush Theatre in 2009 and went on to receive that year's George Devine Award. He is a graduate of the Young Writers' Programme at the Royal Court, where his next play, *Wanderlust*, opened in 2010 and was shortlisted for the *Evening Standard*'s Most Promising Playwright Award. *One Day When We Were Young*, in a Paines Plough and Sheffield Theatres production, was staged at the Crucible Studio Theatre, Sheffield, in 2011, and later transferred to Shoreditch Town Hall as part of the Roundabout Season. *Constellations*, which opened at the Royal Court in 2012 and transferred to the Duke of York's Theatre, won the *Evening Standard* Theatre Award for Best Play. *The Same Deep Water As Me* was staged at the Donmar Warehouse in 2013 and was nominated for an Olivier Award for Best New Comedy. *Blurred Lines* (co-created with director Carrie Cracknell) was staged at The Shed, National Theatre, in 2014. *Incognito*, a co-commission between Nabokov and Live Theatre, Newcastle, toured the UK in 2014.

also by Nick Payne from Faber

IF THERE IS I HAVEN'T FOUND IT YET
WANDERLUST
ONE DAY WHEN WE WERE YOUNG
CONSTELLATIONS
THE SAME DEEP WATER AS ME
INCOGNITO

NICK PAYNE

Elegy

ff

FABER & FABER

First published in 2016
by Faber and Faber Ltd
74–77 Great Russell Street
London WC1B 3DA

First published in the US in 2016

Typeset by Country Setting, Kingsdown, Kent CT14 8ES
Printed in England by CPI Group (UK) Ltd, Croydon CR0 4YY

4 6 8 10 9 7 5 3

Acknowledgements

Professor Deborah Bowman, John Buzzetti, Alastair
Coomer, Barbara Flynn, Ben Hall, Steve King, Kate
Pakenham, Mum, Josie Rourke, Professor Anil Seth,
Tom Scutt, Professor Murray Shanahan, Nina Sosanya,
Zoë Wanamaker, Charlie Weedon, Lily Williams,
Dr Rowan Williams, Dinah Wood and all the staff at
the Donmar Warehouse.

I would like to acknowledge the following books and
their authors: *The Brain is Wider Than the Sky* by Bryan
Appleyard, *Levels of Life* by Julian Barnes, *On Romantic
Love* by Berit Brogaard, *Moonwalking with Einstein: The
Art and Science of Remembering Everything* by Joshua
Foer, *Keeper* by Andrea Gillies, *The Soul of the Marionette*
by John Gray, *Leaving Alexandria*: *A Memoir of Faith
and Doubt* by Richard Holloway, *The Future of the
Mind* by Michio Kaku, *Inventing the Universe: Why
We Can't Stop Talking about Science, Faith and God* by
Alister McGrath, *Stammered Songbook* by Erwin Mortier,
Thirty-Second Brain edited by Anil Seth, *The Technological
Singularity* by Murray Shanahan and *In Defence of
Wonder* by Raymond Tallis.

Elegy was first performed at the Donmar Warehouse, London, on 21 April 2016. The cast, in order of speaking, was as follows:

Carrie Barbara Flynn
Lorna Zoë Wanamaker
Miriam Nina Sosanya

Director Josie Rourke
Designer Tom Scutt
Lighting Designer Paule Constable
Sound Designer Ian Dickinson for Autograph

Characters

Carrie
sixties

Lorna
sixties

Dr Miriam Gomez
forties or above

ELEGY

For Minna, with all my love

Every love story is a potential grief story. If not at first, then later. If not for one, then for the other. Sometimes, for both.

Julian Barnes, *Levels of Life*
(London: Jonathan Cape, 2013), p. 102

As for me, I've arrived, already, at a state of self-protective forgetting. People are good at that, at moving on, dwindling the past into a story we tell ourselves, into parables, and choosing the future over the past.

Andrea Gillies, *Keeper*
(London: Short Books, 2009), p. 357

We yearn for a type of knowledge that would make us other than we are – though what we would like to be, we cannot say.

John Gray, *The Soul of the Marionette*
(London: Allen Lane, 2015), p. 165

SEVEN

Carrie I can tell you how we met if you like.

Lorna If it's useful.

Carrie Is it useful for you, you tell me.

Lorna I meant if it's useful for you. To, I don't know, to talk about it.

Carrie You could ask me questions.

Lorna Questions?

Carrie About us, about anything. You like. Anything you want to know. And if I know –

Lorna But –

Carrie If I know, I'll tell you. I'll answer you.

Lorna I find hearing about the past does me little to no good. But.

Beat.

Carrie We met in church. I was part of a choir. And you were hoping to – You came along, alone, and – You weren't religiously inclined, by the way. If anything the opposite. I was – Well, every, when I'm feeling, every now and again, when I'm feeling particularly . . . We were teachers.

Lorna I know.

Carrie You do?

Lorna I know that I was a teacher.

Carrie You do, sorry.

Lorna I know that much because I can still remember that far back.

Carrie You can, yes.

Lorna The only part that is gone is the last twenty, twenty-five or so years.

Carrie 'The only part' . . .!

Lorna Yes.

Carrie Those years, to me you see, those years are – They're everything.

Lorna Yes.

Carrie What about retiring, do you remember retiring?

Lorna 'Remember' isn't, I don't know, isn't strictly speaking, the right, I don't know. They're not memories any more so there's no hope of me remembering them. Or forgetting them, you know, if you see what I mean.

Carrie Well if you're interested, that is something I can tell you about too.

   Beat.

We started talking to each other in the church because we were both teachers. That was all I meant.

Lorna What do you teach?

Carrie Did.

Lorna What did you teach.

Carrie Religious studies.

Lorna So you are, I don't know, religious then, in some way or other?

Carrie (*beat*) Listen, how are you?

Lorna It –

Carrie Since being discharged, how are you?

Lorna Seems to be going well, I don't know.

Carrie I'm sure it is.

Lorna I had a few speech, a few language, issues, but they seem to be on the wane.

Carrie What does it feel like?

Lorna What does what feel like?

Carrie Not – Having this – Not having a piece of your life – How does that –

Lorna It feels, I don't know. It feels. I don't think I know how to answer that, I'm sorry.

Carrie You never need to apologise.

Lorna I suppose you could say it feels a little like waking up somewhere unfamiliar. You wake up, you look around, unsure, you know, for a moment, where you are. And then, I don't know, the uncertainty disappears and you just get on with it.

Carrie You don't feel you're missing something?

Lorna I'm sorry but what are these questions really about?

Carrie They're not about anything. They're not even really supposed to feel like questions.

Lorna I'm feeling a real weight of expectation –

Carrie I don't expect any –

Lorna I agreed to meet with you –

Carrie I'm sorry – Please –

Lorna People've told me, friends, that you were incredibly good, kind –

Carrie You can go – You don't have to stay –

Lorna Just talk. That's all you have to do.

Carrie Got it.

Lorna Talk to me, you know, stop asking me things.

Carrie I will, okay, but, to clarify, you said a moment ago, you said it would do you 'little to no' –

Lorna I, fine, I don't know, I don't know what you want me to say?

Carrie I don't want you to say, or do, or feel that you have to do anything. I wanted to see you. That was all.

   Beat.

The choir sang at the wedding. You didn't stick it out, the choir, you didn't stay with it. But they were, yeah, arguably some of our closest friends. They sang the first dance. As in we danced while they sang. Rather than having a band, or a – They were, a cappella, unaccompanied, and we were dancing.

Lorna What did they sing?

Carrie 'Mirrorball'.

   Lorna seemingly doesn't know it.

You didn't really want it. But it was the first dance at my parents' wedding. You said, yeah, you said it was too sentimental. But it reminded me of them, my parents.

Lorna You were at your parents' wedding?

8

Carrie No, I – Sorry – As in, I meant, I've seen the footage. Retrospectively. (*Sings, soft, fragile.*) 'Down to you, de–ar.'

No, Lorna doesn't know it. Beat.

There were readings, too, as well, there were some readings. 'A Scattering' was yours and then 'Wedding' was mine. And we –

Lorna (*does remember/know 'A Scattering'*) Which one? From 'Scattering', which one –

Carrie 'Scattering', it was the, the poem itself. All the ones, all your suggestions were really morbid . . .! They were all about death. Or dying. Or, yeah, people being widowed. Illness. And I said, I said, people are going to think we're willing this thing to fail. But you said, you said death and marriage go hand in hand. You start, the start is about, you commit because of death, not, yeah, not – If more people started thinking about death sooner you said, we'd all fuck up a lot less.

Lorna I don't know.

Carrie Well, it's what you said. 'Wedding' is beautiful, by the way. If you don't remem— (*Corrects herself.*) If you don't know it, then you should, yeah – I have a copy in fact. If you –

Lorna Is there anything you want from me?

Carrie . . . Want?

Lorna I don't know, yes, is there something specific?

Carrie There are lots of things I want from you.

Lorna But is there anything in particular I can help you with?

Carrie You could let me kiss you.

9

A flicker of irritation from Lorna.

That was a joke.

Lorna I think that would be, you know, I wouldn't say I'm particularly comfortable with that.

Carrie I want to love you, if that's what you mean. That's what I miss, how about that, I miss *loving* you, I miss *actually loving you*. In some ways, the irony of all this, is that if you *had* died – Because it's as if you are dead, because you look at me as if I'm a ghost. But there you are, it's you, in front of me. And I remember, I remember every single last fucking there is.

Lorna That sounds like a threat.

Carrie What?

Lorna Wishing I was dead –

Carrie No, I wasn't –

Lorna I am, I don't know, sorry for you, you know, in a way. You clearly, I don't know, you put a lot into – All this – Helping me – But I don't, fine, no I don't see anything when I look at you. It's like glass, it's like a pane of glass. There's half a reflection maybe, but it doesn't mean anything to me. And in a way, I don't know, I think that's probably better. Because if I did – see something – then we'd know something was wrong. We'd know something hadn't worked. Look, there's an issue in that we're still married.

'Married' might hang in the air for a moment or two.

Carrie . . . Fuck . . .

Lorna I don't know how to put it, you know . . .

Carrie Jesus.

Lorna It can wait. It's not *per se* urgent. But I think it would be cleaner –

Carrie 'Cleaner'?

Lorna Yes.

Carrie That is a horrible – 'Cleaner' – That is such a horrible –

Lorna Neater, I don't know, more straightforward –

Carrie Maybe you were right, maybe I should kill you, take all your money, keep all our things.

    Beat.

That was a joke, come on, that was so clearly –

Lorna It wasn't funny.

Carrie You used to make jokes like that all the –

Lorna I'm not that person.

Carrie Well, you look pretty fucking similar to me.

    Beat.

You're the person you are when I met you. No? You're that person. Because that's where they set you back to. No?

Lorna I don't know.

Carrie Stop saying that, Christ! (*Beat.*) I want to help, I'm sorry, of course I want to help. I'll do whatever you need.

Lorna Thank you.

    Beat.

Carrie If I want to contact you again how should I do that?

Lorna Through the, the same as this time would be good for me, via the solicitor.

Carrie What about the LPA?

Lorna I don't know. Given I'm still alive, I assume it's null and void. But.

Beat.

Carrie I nearly had octopus last night, would you believe.

She was hoping this might mean something to Lorna, but seemingly it doesn't. Beat. Carrie looks right at Lorna, who holds her gaze.

I was apoplectic when the hospital said I couldn't see you any more.

Lorna says nothing.

They really did take it all, didn't they?

Lorna And thank God they did. Because I am better. I have a life. I have a life now.

SIX

Miriam You know what, let's move on.

Carrie Yeah, I think that's a, because yeah, if I'm honest –

Miriam (*moving them on*) Lorna has requested – I've had a request from Lorna – Lorna has requested that you no longer – that you cease visitations. Your visitations cease. Indefinitely.

Carrie (*beat*) Why?

Miriam Lorna, she feels, in the build-up to being discharged, she feels she wants to keep her previous, she feels she now wants to focus on her life going forward.

Carrie This request was made to you?

Miriam It was.

Carrie Directly to you?

Miriam It was.

Carrie What about the, about the, the other, the rest – She said that?

Miriam Said what, sorry?

Carrie Not seeing me.

Miriam The request came directly from Lorna, that's correct. In the build-up to being discharged –

Carrie She was upset? What, by my visits?

Miriam You know what I think, it was a combination of factors.

Carrie Fuck off a combination. That was so obviously a yes-or-no-straight-answer question.

Miriam I can only pass on what I was asked to pass on.

Carrie Or you can take some responsibility. You can take some responsibility and be upfront with me.

Miriam Once Lorna is discharged, there will be a period of recovery. Of transition. Aftercare. Which will involve a variety of different, a very intensive, particular –

Carrie I can help with that.

Miriam Okay.

Carrie I can help her, in a, with the, in a no-strings-attached capacity I can help.

Miriam Would you like me to relay that to Lorna?

Carrie Yes. Yes, I would.

Miriam Then okay, then, you know what, I will.

Carrie But what do you think? What do you think this is about?

Miriam You know what, speaking honest, speaking honestly with you, we see this a lot. I've had, I've seen patients leave their families, give up their jobs. Big, big changes in lifestyle. It's a second chance. (*Beat.*) People respond, people . . . recover in all manner of different – Not to mention at each *stage* of the – Lorna might feel a particular way at this particular point in time. But it might not reflect how she feels in the longer term.

Carrie Are you saying I'll be stopped?

Miriam Stopped?

Carrie If I try to visit.

Miriam The hospital will respect the wishes of the patient.

Carrie You'll throw me out?

Miriam I personally won't be responsible –

Carrie I know, I know, I'm not saying, I'm not saying you, I'm saying –

Miriam If Lorna, if she feels in any way, let's say, if she feels in any way uncomfortable, or –

Carrie I have Lasting Power of Attorney.

Miriam I'm passing on Lorna's request, that's all I can do.

Carrie Will you tell her that I would like to see her again.

Miriam Okay.

Carrie Will you tell her that her that, yeah, that I would like to sit with her again.

Miriam Okay.

Carrie Sit down with her and have a conversation.

Miriam I will.

Carrie Will she be seeing her family still? Nieces, nephews.

Miriam (*beat*) Carrie, would you mind if I say something to you? And you know what, I'm saying this to you off the record. You have, the decision you undertook has saved, preserved, Lorna's life. Without this procedure, the disease would have taken her life from her. It would have robbed her, unequivocally, of the, it would have taken who she is, or was, it would have taken that from her. Slowly and painfully and without remorse. And you have supported Lorna at every stage, with a grace and a dignity that is – And that, now, that commitment, that drive to save, to prevent this illness, this disease, the drive to ensure – That is what we now have to focus on. I would suggest. We have to allow Lorna the autonomy, give her the agency, to decide who she now wishes to be. Right or wrong, for better or worse.

Carrie Giving someone autonomy after you've hijacked a not insignificant amount of their, fucking, seems to me to be somewhat of a contradiction in terms.

Miriam You said it yourself, it was Lorna's wish that you have Lasting Power of Attorney.

Carrie I swear I'm gonna burn this fucking place to the ground.

Beat.

I won't, that was, obviously that is not something I actually intend to do.

Miriam Carrie – And I think we may have touched on this briefly at one point, but – I wonder, have you thought about – Because there are a variety, a wide variety, of, for people in your position – Support.

Carrie Therapy, you're talking about –

Miriam I recently worked with, a priest, a parish priest – And this particular patient had asked us to remove – There had been, the patient –

Carrie The priest.

Miriam Had been responsible for a, an accident. A pile-up. And he couldn't, he wrestled, but he couldn't comprehend, he, as he put it – He couldn't live with himself. So the team and I, we went back, right back, as per his wishes, and removed any instance, any exhibition of, or behaviour tied to – Long-term, short-term –

Carrie I don't understand?

Miriam His faith.

Carrie My head is about to – You removed his –

Miriam His faith, yes.

Carrie I don't believe that is something you can have actually –

Miriam The point – One or two members of his congregation were set completely adrift –

Carrie *(interrupting on 'One or two')* Yeah no I'm serious because this is the problem. Isn't it? It's this – distinction. Or something. Between what you think you did and what you *actually* did. You can't take away someone's – Because that isn't how it – Taking all the bits doesn't mean you took the, the thing itself. Because all the, all the bits, all the bits add up to something far greater, I mean, my God, far greater than –

Miriam We can help. There is help available. That was all I wanted to convey to you, Carrie.

Carrie You've done – I don't want your – Makes me shudder, thinking about, talking, like this. As if what happens to us doesn't mean anything. As if we don't learn from it, 's if it doesn't matter. I may never see Lorna again. We may never – But loving her has *unquestionably* – And I am not prepared to have you, splice me open and, plug me in or whatever the – I want this.

Miriam I wasn't suggesting –

Carrie This is real and I want it.

Miriam But look at how we treat pain. As a –

Carrie I'm sorry, what?

Miriam We treat the symptoms of physical pain all the time, without so much as a – A patient comes into the hospital, let's say, with a very severe – Should we deprive them of pain relief because it might rob them of the full emotional experience?

Carrie You're not –

Miriam Of the ability to learn from their mistake?

Carrie You're not comparing –

Miriam What we do here is in many ways akin –

Carrie But –

Miriam Forgetting is one of the most beneficial processes we possess –

Carrie Enough, enough –

Miriam Okay –

Carrie Stop, please, stop.

Miriam Okay, all right, I won't –

Carrie I made a horrible, fucking, terrible, fucking, we don't need to keep . . .

She is upset. Beat.

Will you tell her that I would like to see her again. Please. But that if she doesn't, I'll respect her, if she doesn't want to, see me, then yeah, then of course I'll respect that.

Miriam You know what, despite what you may think of me, of the work that I do, I am sorry, Carrie.

Carrie When is she being discharged?

FIVE

Miriam And any head pain?

Lorna shakes her head.

Nausea?

Lorna shakes her head.

Nothing at all?

Lorna Nothing.

Miriam Great. And how have you been getting on with the Myelinitol?

Lorna No, fine.

Miriam And what about the Symmetrel?

Lorna Same. Fine.

Miriam Is there anything you would like to ask me?

Lorna I don't know.

Beat.

Maybe you could explain what the stuff I'm taking does again?

Miriam You bet.

Lorna I thought I understood, but, I don't know, maybe I'm, I'm not sure I did.

Miriam Why don't we start, let's start with the Symmetrel. Which is a receptor antagonist. It attacks, or blocks, the over-production of a particular kind of neurotransmitter.

Glutamate. Which causes cell damage. Which in turn impairs the brain's ability to recover. To repair.

Lorna . . . Okay . . .

Miriam Alongside the Symmetrel, we also, the reason we have you taking Myelinitol, is because Myelinitol is a myelin stimulant.

Lorna Myelin?

Miriam Yes, Myelin is the, is a white matter, which coats, or rather insulates, axons from other nearby axons. Dramatically increasing the speed –

Lorna Sorry, and, an axon is a –

Miriam A long, thinnish fibre which extends between the cell body, what we call the soma, of a neuron, right the way across, enabling the transmission of information from neuron to neuron. And myelination –

Lorna (*wrapping her head around the word*) Mye–lin–ation.

Miriam Myelination is the process whereby these axons, these fibres, are coated, protecting and strengthening axons, which in turn protects the strength of the signals being transmitted. Meaning any new relationships, new connections, between either recovering neural pathways or indeed previously unconnected neural pathways –

Lorna (*it's fucking baffling*) Maybe I don't, after all, maybe we don't need to go over the – It's quite a lot to try and –

Miriam I'm sorry.

Lorna No.

Miriam We're rebuilding.

Lorna And what, if it, if the rebuilding doesn't work . . . ?

Miriam The treatment has never not worked.

Lorna But, for the sake of argument, I don't know, what happens, if it doesn't? And it comes back?

Miriam You mean if the –

Lorna If I become ill again, if the disease, if –

Miriam That has never happened.

Lorna Hypothetically –

Miriam You know what, it's hard for me to speak hypothetically because what you're asking me is such an unknown –

Lorna That's why it's a hypothetical, because I'm asking you to –

Miriam Okay, well, let's say, during a check-up, during an examination, let's say in six months time, we find signs of deterioration. New signs of fresh deterioration –

Lorna That's what I'm asking you.

Miriam (*beat*) Lorna, is there something the matter?

Lorna I think, I don't know, I think I – I thought that I had had a dream. But it was, I don't know, I don't know how to explain it. I don't think it was a dream, I think it was a memory. Of, of the lady –

Miriam Carrie.

Lorna Yes, the lady who –

Miriam Carrie.

Lorna We were, we were, rotating.

Miriam Okay.

Lorna Close. She was, we were incredibly close.

Miriam Okay.

Lorna Incredibly close together. Rotating in circles together. There was a large group of people singing. It was like a burst, a shock, the image itself. It was, I don't know, it was, for a flicker of a second, and then –

Miriam Okay, you know what –

Lorna Can you check, is there a way of checking?

Miriam I'm not sure I understand –

Lorna Checking what it was that I saw.

Miriam I can tell you now, Lorna, it will not have been a memory.

Lorna But how can you, you can't know, how can you say that?

Miriam Lorna, I know there is a lot, happening, at the moment, to take on board –

Lorna You're not listening to me! You're not, you're not listening to what I'm –

Miriam Okay –

Lorna I'm asking you to check, that's all.

Miriam You're right. You're right. We can investigate. We ought to be able to look into it, you're right.

Lorna Thank you.

Miriam Leave it with me.

Lorna That sounds – Thank you.

Miriam Are you sure everything is all right, you're feeling all right?

Lorna Do you think I can trust her?

Miriam You mean –

Lorna Carrie, the lady –

Miriam I'm not sure I understand the question?

Lorna Is she honest? Is she to be taken at her word?

Miriam It's, you have to understand, it isn't really for me to comment on whether or not –

Lorna But you know her better than me, in the circumstances, you must, don't you, you must have a view?

Miriam Lorna, it would be, you have to understand –

Lorna Did she love me?

Miriam (*beat*) Why do you want to know –

Lorna Because.

Miriam Why is it important to you at this stage –

Lorna Because I'm wondering if I ought to see her again.

Beat.

Miriam It's very difficult for me to say with any certainty whether Carrie –

Lorna Your opinion, your view, that's all I want.

Miriam It's difficult, Lorna, not because I have any doubts, *per se*, over whether or not Carrie, might, but, it's difficult because love, so-called, the experience we term love –

Lorna I didn't realise it would be so complicated . . .!

Miriam Love isn't a physical or chemical element. It's a partially conscious state of the mind. And as we know the brain creates the mind, so in order –

Lorna I don't know what you're saying, I don't –

Miriam From a neurological point of view, love affects the brain like, for example, anger, or fear, or grief. Like cocaine. You take a hit, and it lights up. The amygdala, you remember we talked about the, it's the almond-shaped, the epicentre of fear, and some would say, though I'm sceptical myself, that falling in love sends the amygdala haywire, but –

Lorna Hold on, this is, is ridiculous. Isn't it? Either she does or doesn't, how can you –

Miriam Carrie would certainly attest to loving you, yes. But as to whether or not that may be true, it's impossible – I can look at the available evidence and deliver the most likely hypothesis, for example, but I don't – Because if I can't tell you *what* something is, then I certainly can't testify to its existence.

Lorna Well that is, wow, that is – I don't even know what to say to that.

Miriam Science, the work that I do, is a method of inquiry, not a view of the world, Lorna. Right or wrong, for better or worse.

Lorna What about your children, your family?

Miriam What about them?

Lorna When they tell you they love you do you stop them and sit them down and tell them, stupid little almond brains hooked on crack, sorry kids, it's a sham, it's all a fucking hoodwink –

Miriam Lorna, Lorna: I need you to calm down. All right?

Beat.

Lorna I think, the way she looks at me, I don't know, I think that she is sincere.

Miriam says nothing.

24

And, now, what if, I don't know, I could, I could get to know her all over again.

Miriam You can do anything. And we can help you.

Lorna I feel sorry for her, how do you explain that?

Miriam Well, empathy –

Lorna That was rhetorical, it was a rhetorical, I don't actually –

Miriam Okay –

Lorna No more, no more science.

Miriam 'zips' her mouth, perhaps.

What would you do if you were me, if you were me in this situation, what would you do?

Miriam You know what, I would focus on my recovery.

FOUR

Carrie Tell me again.

Miriam Okay. Nano—

Carrie Again how it would work.

Miriam Nanobots are administered via an injection. From the information gathered, from this information, we are then able to construct an exact working replica of a particular brain. A holistic, real-time simulation which recreates all the electrochemical activity of a particular – Every neuron, every connection –

Carrie So everything, it's, you're able to see –

Miriam We are able to see, yes. Everything. Particular patterns of activity. Particular neurons, particular regions even, that may have been severely affected by the –

Carrie And once you've, once you've got this, demo, this, you –

Miriam We then, the team and I, take a meeting to decide upon our recommendations. In Lorna's case –

Carrie Yes.

Miriam Though of course we won't know for certain until –

Carrie No, yeah, no sure, but –

Miriam We would, I would suspect, be looking at discussing some kind of neural prosthesis. Depending on the scale of the damage wrought by the disease, that might involve replacing neurons with synthetic – Or, more likely, in Lorna's –

Carrie Yes.

Miriam It might involve the removal and replacement of a particular area, or a particular network of neurons –

Carrie And once you, once you've removed – Once it's gone, it's, yeah it's just – Gone?

Miriam The disease you mean, or the –

Carrie No, the stuff, the memories, all the stuff that comes out with the bits you have to remove –

Miriam In removing the disease – in order to ensure the removal of the disease in its entirety, we, yes – Anything associated, any memories associated with anything that is removed will, yes, will also be removed.

Carrie And how much is that, by now, by this, at this point?

Miriam doesn't entirely understand the question.

How many years are we talking? Infected, diseased –

Miriam It's – Memory doesn't function in a linear fashion. Memories can be formed, can be, across several areas –

Carrie But you can see, no? From the map, from the simulation, you can see exactly –

Miriam I see, sorry, yes, I see what you mean now – Yes, from the simulation we would be able to ascertain what would be lost.

Carrie So you know, from the first scan, that first map, when Lorna was diagnosed, you know –

Miriam Yes, I see.

Carrie That's what I'm asking. A ballpark, if you had to –

Miriam To answer your question exactly, in any sort of meaningful –

Carrie I'm not asking for exactly. That's not what I'm asking for.

Miriam There, from memory, from the information we gathered in order to diagnose, from that replica . . . Fifteen, perhaps twenty, perhaps thirty years appeared to be –

Carrie You mean the *last* twenty to thirty years, or you mean –

Miriam It isn't as straightforward as – I worry we're in real danger of reducing an extremely complex –

Carrie No, I know, I know, I get – I get that. I do. This isn't about holding you to ransom to some figure. Some figure you're about to give me, some number. This is about – I have to make a decision. I have to. And before, fucking, before I – I just. I just want to know everything you know. Or as much of it as you feel, yeah as you feel able to –

Miriam The disease won't progress in a linear fashion. And, as you know, nor is memory a linear process. We aren't – Things aren't stored. They can't be uploaded or downloaded. But, yes, at the moment, from what I can remember, the damage caused by the disease seemed to be primarily focused around, associated with the last, more recent past events, namely the last ten, perhaps fifteen, perhaps twenty – Perhaps more.

Carrie Years?

Miriam But there were, and this is important, there were several exceptions, several memories from elsewhere in –

Carrie But to be completely, just to be – If we do nothing, eventually, yeah eventually, it'll just . . . If we do nothing she'll just . . .

Miriam We talked previously about the different stages and, yes, in the final stage Lorna will likely have difficulty talking, walking, eating. Incontinence. Delusions, hallucinations, possibly. Fear, anger, aggression. There are no rules, every patient I have ever worked with, over the years, has presented with a, a different cocktail of symptoms –

Carrie And if we do do this, if we do do it, it goes, the disease, that's it, she recovers?

Miriam It's a long process, involving, you know what, involving a great deal –

Carrie Yes or no, I need a yes or no. She will, or she won't recover. In your view. On this day, at this moment in time.

Miriam The procedure's success rate speaks for itself.

Carrie Fuck. (*Beat.*) We met in our, fucking – We'd lived entire, other lives. Before we met. In our forties. We met in our, fucking, forties. So she, yeah, she won't know who I am. She won't recognise me.

Miriam Correct.

Carrie Because you will have taken, you will have removed . . .

Miriam That's correct.

Carrie You know, don't you, she had real, we had a long, before she got really bad, when she was still able to – We had this long, drawn out, and she has real doubts. Christ.

Miriam Carrie, would you mind if I say something to you?

Carrie shakes her head.

For years, when I was training, during my training, the opposition to the work that I was interested in – Playing

God, people would say. It's unnatural. You're tampering, you've not, what right do you have – And I nearly stopped, I nearly gave up on it all. And then like so many of us, when my – Because it's all very well in the abstract, it's all very well being oppositional when you haven't – But when you have, when you have been through it, when you have had to look someone, someone you love, when you've had to watch them as they, the indignity of it all, once – It becomes impossible to look away. The work we do here, what we now know about the brain, hosts of intractable diseases, the dementias, Parkinson's, schizophrenia, bipolar, depression – All understood. All treatable. And all curable. Over a hundred billion neurons and there isn't a single one of them –

Carrie Yeah I get it. I get it. I get it. But it's all so cruel, isn't it, all this, pathways and removing and extracting, it's gruelling – How about you tell me how to, fucking, *cope* for fuck's sake, how about you tell me how I'm s'posed to do that . . .?!

   Beat.

Will anything remain? Anything of me? And I'm not talking about memory, not talking about, I'm talking about – Any feeling. Any feelings toward me. Somewhere, some ghost.

THREE

Lorna I'm sorry, I don't know where I am.

Carrie It doesn't matter.

Lorna I'm sorry.

Carrie It doesn't matter.

Lorna I was looking for a cup.

Carrie Cup?

Lorna I was looking for the –

Carrie We have plenty of cups at home.

Lorna No, I was looking for the cup.

Carrie Which cup, you tell me, and we'll go and find it.

Lorna No, I don't mean, I'm not – Ah fuck it.

Carrie I'm listening.

Lorna No, I don't know. I thought we were choosing. Choosing the readings, for the . . . But now I don't know.

Carrie What readings?

Lorna Fucking thing.

Carrie Shall we go home now?

Lorna I'm sorry.

Carrie You don't need to be.

Lorna I'm so sorry.

Carrie Darling, listen to me –

Lorna You're so good to me.

Carrie Book, do you mean book?

Lorna Yes!

Carrie You were looking for a book?

Lorna What? Yes. I think so. No, I don't know.

Carrie Is that why you came all the way here?

Lorna This is such a beautiful place.

Carrie It is.

Lorna It's my favourite shop.

Carrie Shall we go home now?

Lorna *Right, reckon I've got it, found it, this is the one.*

Carrie *Is it morbid?*

Lorna *A bit, but what's wrong with morbid?*

Carrie *Is it about death?*

Lorna *Will you let me read it to you?*

Carrie *I will.*

Lorna
'Day by nomadic day
Our anniversaries go by,
Dates anchored in an inner sky,
To utmost ground, interior clay.
It was September blue –'

Carrie Lorna.

Lorna 'When I walked with you first, my love –'

Carrie Lorna. Lorna.

Lorna is adrift.

Shall we go back inside?

Lorna I'm sorry.

Carrie I don't mind, I'd just like us to go back inside.

Lorna You're angry.

Carrie It's very late.

Lorna Don't get angry with me.

Carrie Darling, it's really cold out here.

Lorna Don't get fucking angry with me.

Carrie I'm not.

Lorna Don't talk to me like that.

Carrie I wasn't talking to you like anything.

Lorna Fuck me if I'm not trying, Carrie.

Carrie I know.

Lorna You don't know what this is like.

Carrie Then let me help.

Lorna Fuck . . .

Carrie Can we go back inside?

Lorna I'm sorry.

Carrie I know, I understand, you don't need to apologise.

Lorna I don't know what's happening.

Carrie You have a disease, you're ill. That's what's happening. We know that.

Lorna God, it's fucking awful all this.

Carrie I know.

Lorna Isn't it?

Carrie It is.

Lorna Fucking at sea, all this.

Carrie I know, it's awful, it's shit. It's a shitty disease.

Lorna I'm sorry.

Carrie Me too.

Lorna *It's called 'A Scattering'.*

Carrie *Christ don't tell me –*

Lorna *Will you –*

Carrie *Scattering, ashes, death, urns, funerals –*

Lorna *Will you let me read it to you.*

Carrie *Love, listen, I'm really really sorry, but I'm just not sure I want to hear –*

Lorna *It's beautiful I promise you, it's beautiful.*

Carrie *Is it about death?*

Lorna *It's about everything.*

   Beat.

'I expect you've seen the footage: elephants,
   Finding the bones of their own kind –'

Carrie *Jesus, Lorna –*

Lorna
   '– dropped by the wayside, picked clean by scavengers
   and the sun, then untidily left there
   decide to do something about it.'

Carrie *It's a no.*

Lorna
   'But what, exactly? They can't, of course,
   Reassemble the old elephant magnificence –'

34

Carrie *I've heard enough, please, come on. Who wants to hear about dead elephants at their –*

Lorna Let me finish!

Carrie Finish what?

Lorna Stop interrupting me.

Carrie I haven't.

Lorna Fucking, you fucking –

Carrie Lorna, please –

Lorna Bitch, fucking, how dare you?

Carrie Please, calm down.

Lorna Who the fuck do you think you are? Huh?

Carrie You need to stop shouting.

Lorna You can't, don't you dare, you can't tell me what to do. Fuck do you think you are? You Need To Start – Listening – To me. To me. Understood?

Carrie I'd like to take you home. All right? That's all I want to do.

Lorna *Can I get to the end? Please. I'm sorry. I know it's a bit morbid, you're right, it is a bit, but the ending – God, it's just one of my favourites. Please.*

Carrie *I'm listening.*

Lorna
'That day will still exist
Long after I have joined you where
Rings radiate the dusty air
And bangles bind each powdered wrist.
Here comes that day again.
What shall I do? Instruct me, dear,
Longanimous encourager –'

Carrie *Big word.*

Lorna
   'Sweet soul in the athletic rain
   And wife now to the weather.'

What do you think?

Carrie *It is really beautiful –*

Lorna *See!*

Carrie *But it is in the end about someone's dead wife.*

Lorna *I know, I know, but –*

Carrie *Also I'm not sure I know what long . . . ani . . .?*

Lorna *Longanimous.*

Carrie *Yeah, what is that?*

Lorna *It means, long-suffering, it means, resilient,*
endurance.

Carrie *Cheery.*

Lorna
   'Long after I have joined you where
   Rings radiate the dusty air
   And bangles bind each powdered wrist' is fucking
   beautiful, Carrie.

Carrie *It is. No question. Why don't we put it on the*
list?

Lorna *I think we should.*

Carrie *Then let's do that.*

Lorna Can we stop?

Carrie Stop?

Lorna . . .

Carrie Stop what?

Lorna I don't know, sorry, I thought we were . . .

Carrie Shall we go back to bed?

Lorna Yeah, sorry, I don't know what's . . .

Carrie It really doesn't matter. As long as you're all right.

Lorna Well, I'm not all right I'm fucking dying, but –

Carrie I meant in the short term.

Lorna I know you did, I was being 'humorous'.

Carrie Is that what it was?

Lorna What are we going to do?

Carrie I promise to make more of an effort to find you amusing.

Lorna In the long term, I'm being serious.

Carrie Do we have to be serious right now?

Lorna Seems as good a time as any.

Carrie What are we going to do about what?

Lorna My ailing mind.

Carrie I'm going to be your longanimous encourager.

Lorna No I'm the longanimous encourager. The dead wife is the longanimous encourager.

Carrie Who says?

Lorna You're sidestepping.

Carrie I don't know what you want me to say.

Lorna It's going to get much worse.

Carrie I know.

Lorna I'll be a shitting pissing mess.

Carrie So what?

Lorna I wouldn't want to look after you if you were a shitting pissing mess.

Carrie Well then, it's a good thing I'm not you.

Lorna Carrie –

Carrie What are you doing, why are you talking about this –

Lorna Because –

Carrie Talking like this –

Lorna Because –

Carrie I know it's going to be God-awful, the stuff of fucking nightmares, last thing I need is you rubbing it in my face, thank you very much –

Lorna I'm not rubbing it in your face, I'm trying to have a serious conversation.

Carrie Well then, yeah, maybe I don't, maybe I'm not ready to have that discussion.

Lorna What about a double suicide?

Carrie Fuck off, Lorna, that isn't even –

Lorna It's a joke, I come in peace, it was a joke.

Carrie *All right I think I've got one.*

Lorna *Really?*

Carrie *I think, yeah, I mean I think so.*

Lorna *What's it called?*

Carrie *It's called 'Wedding'.*

Lorna *Isn't that a bit on the nose?*

Carrie *Listen.*

Lorna *Where is it taken from?*

Carrie *A book.*

Lorna *Yes but which book?*

Carrie *It's from an anthology.*

Lorna *It's not a poem you know?*

Carrie *I found it in a, don't be such a snob.*

Lorna *I think the readings should mean something.*

Carrie *Shut up and listen.*

Lorna I've cut myself.

Carrie What?

Lorna I've cut myself.

Carrie Where?

Lorna I've cut myself.

Carrie Let me see.

   Beat.

Lorna. Can I see, can I look?

Lorna I'm sorry, I don't know where I am.

Carrie You're home.

Lorna I'm really petrified, Carrie.

Carrie Yes.

Lorna What?

Carrie Yes I know you are.

Lorna And you, what are you up to?

Carrie I'm afraid as well.

Lorna Would you like to go?

Carrie Go?

Lorna Leave, leave me.

Carrie What on earth are you talking about?

Lorna Eventually it won't make any difference anyway.

Carrie Lorna, come on –

Lorna I won't be able to tell the difference eventually.

Carrie Enough, all right, that's enough.

Lorna This is the closing-down sale.

Carrie You're being an idiot.

Lorna Last chance.

Carrie Shut up, what's the matter with you, I'm not going anywhere.

Lorna Then get ready to watch me dwindle away.

Carrie Stop talking.

Lorna Are you, though, are you ready for that?

Carrie Lorna –

Lorna Are you though?

Carrie Yes.

Lorna You are?

Carrie Yes!

Lorna Hollow shell –

Carrie I don't care.

Lorna Give it time.

Carrie You're being an idiot.

Lorna You'll look back, you'll look back on this moment –

Carrie Shut the –

Lorna You will, you watch, you'll look back, and you'll think –

Carrie Lorna –

Lorna And think, you'll think: why didn't I take her up on her offer?

Carrie I'm gonna throw something at you.

Lorna Should've gone, should've left you'll be saying to yourself –

Carrie What is the matter with you?! Stop it! Stop talking! FUCK.

Lorna grows upset. Beat.

Do you want me to read it to you or not?

Lorna What?

Carrie *Shall I read it to you?*

Lorna I do.

Carrie
   'From time to time our love is like a sail
   and when the sail begins to alternate
   from tack to tack, it's like a swallowtail
   and when the swallow flies it's like a coat;
   and if the coat is yours, it has a tear
   like a wide mouth and when the mouth begins
   to draw the wind, it's like a trumpeter
   and when the trumpet blows, it blows like millions –'

Lorna *This doesn't make any sense.*

Carrie
'and this, my love, when millions come and go
beyond the need of us, is like a trick;
and when the trick begins, it's like a toe
tip-toeing on a rope, which is like luck;
and when the luck begins –

Lorna What are you doing?

Carrie
                              it's like a wedding,
which is like love, which is like –'

Lorna What are you doing?

Carrie What?

Lorna Just now, what were you doing?

Carrie I was praying.

Lorna Why?

Carrie Please don't take the piss out of me.

Lorna I am not. I want to know.

Carrie I'm frightened.

Lorna What are you frightened about?

Carrie What do you think?

Lorna What are you after?

Carrie What?

Lorna Is there something specific you're after? From you-know-who.

Carrie This and that. Bit of guidance.

Lorna And? Has you-know-who been at all forthcoming?

Carrie I asked you not to take the piss.

Lorna And I am not.

Carrie The conversation is somewhat one-way at the moment.

Lorna That's a shame.

Carrie Maybe.

Lorna What are you going to do?

Carrie Keep at it.

Lorna *Can I hear that last little bit again?*

Carrie *Which bit?*

Lorna *The bit from tip-toe something-something.*

Carrie
*'and when the trick begins, it's like a toe
tip-toeing on a rope, which is like luck;
and when the luck begins, it's like a wedding,
which is like love, which is like everything.'*

What's the verdict?

Beat.

Lorna. Lorna.

Lorna I'm sorry. I don't know where I am.

Carrie is exhausted.

Carrie I can't do this. I'm sorry I can't do this . . .

TWO

Lorna I want it to be you.

Carrie You're sure?

Lorna What do you mean?

Carrie What about your niece?

Lorna We're married.

Carrie I'm asking what about Claire, that's all.

Lorna I can ask Claire if you don't want to do it.

Carrie You can have more than one attorney.

Lorna If you don't want me to appoint you, Carrie –

Carrie All I want –

Lorna Why you would rather it be someone else is beyond –

Carrie You won't have to live with the fallout.

Lorna I'm a burden.

Carrie No.

Lorna My illness is a burden.

Carrie No, you're not listening –

Lorna My faith in you is unwavering.

Carrie 'Faith'?

Lorna Is this a joke to you?

Carrie Unwavering is the opposite of faith.

44

Lorna What?

Carrie We're veering off course.

Lorna I want to know what you said just now means.

Carrie You're trying to start a war –

Lorna At least I'm still trying.

Carrie Fuck you, Lorna.

Lorna There you go, here we go.

Carrie I have faith *because* I waver, not –

Lorna Meaning.

Carrie I need it, I don't necessarily want it, but I –

Lorna And me you.

Carrie I understand that.

Lorna I'm going to need you to remind me who I am.

Carrie But what if –

Lorna And when I don't know who you are any more, I'm going to need you even more.

Carrie And if I can't?

Lorna You will.

Carrie I'm selfish –

Lorna You're not –

Carrie I'm not good enough.

Lorna You are.

Carrie And if I want to save you?

Lorna You can't.

Carrie I can, you know I can. The procedure.

Lorna We agreed.

Carrie We did.

Lorna We agreed to forget about that.

Carrie But when you're gone, when you're not you, what if I change my mind?

Lorna Why would you do that?

Carrie Because the alternative –

Lorna No, the alternative –

Carrie I would rather you have a life –

Lorna But it wouldn't be –

Carrie A life without me, but a life nonetheless.

Lorna There is no life without you.

Carrie But you won't know, you won't be able to tell the difference.

Lorna I am telling you, now, in no uncertain, that is not what I want, Carrie.

Carrie But –

Lorna Do we need to go over it all again?

Carrie No –

Lorna Do not resuscitate.

Carrie You're not –

Lorna Do not alter the very fabric of my being.

Carrie Can we –

Lorna And do not put me into any kind – of, no matter how bad –

Carrie But –

46

Lorna Are we clear?

Carrie I can't make that promise. Those promises, I can't.

Lorna It isn't a promise, it is a legally binding –

Carrie Then it's too much. You're asking too much of me.

Lorna It's the bare minimum, Carrie! (*Beat.*) Look, if this LPA is going to be too much –

Carrie Don't spin this around.

Lorna No, maybe you were right, maybe Claire –

Carrie Don't you dare –

Lorna No, you were, you were right to question –

Carrie Listen –

Lorna I can't pretend I'm not disappointed, but –

Carrie This love isn't a promise one way or the other. It can't –

Lorna Well, that doesn't mean anything.

Carrie I can't promise to watch you, to watch you, fail, to watch you, descend, I can't promise that. To watch you collapse, to plummet – It would be inhumane, to watch you, when there is an alternative. Why would I do that? Why would I do that? To you, why would I do that?

Lorna You're asking me.

Carrie Yes.

Lorna You're asking me –

Carrie If this were the other way around –

Lorna I would obey your wishes.

Carrie Bullshit.

Lorna I would submit –

Carrie No you wouldn't.

Lorna I would follow your instructions to the –

Carrie Let me die?

Lorna You don't 'let' death –

Carrie Oh come on, don't give me that, don't give me –

Lorna It's going to happen whether we like it or not.

Carrie In this particular instance –

Lorna You're scared –

Carrie In this particular instance we happen to have –

Lorna Look at me –

Carrie We have an opportunity to choose 'or not'.

Lorna And then what?

Carrie We do it all over again.

Lorna It's that simple.

Carrie Yes. It happened once –

Lorna Exactly.

Carrie Exactly, it happened once –

Lorna No, exactly, it happened – Why would I want to contemplate – I wouldn't want this again because this means so much to me right now. This is it, all there is. And all this talk of, of, of – It isn't a cure, it's a *myth*. This isn't progress. It's the slip, it's a –

Carrie It could save your life.

Lorna What life? If it isn't saving this life, and this after all is the only life I want –

Carrie But –

Lorna I won't have this life hacked away, chopped up, do you understand?

Carrie But there will come a time, do *you* understand, when you will be begging me, you will, you will be begging and wailing and crying, and pleading with me to save you. Because you will be able to sense it, when the body starts to fall apart –

Lorna No.

Carrie And what will I do then?

Lorna Exactly as you have been instructed.

Carrie What sort of a wife, partner, friend, would I be if I watched you curl up and suffer, knowing full well –

Lorna You have my permission to go.

Carrie What?

Lorna You're right, when it gets that bad –

Carrie I don't want –

Lorna You can leave.

Carrie Be reasonable, for Christ's sake!

Lorna No. I'm dying, I'm allowed to be unreasonable every now and again.

Carrie What is that, is that supposed to be, what is that?

Lorna Look at me. Look at me.

    Carrie does so.

This feels reasonable, *feels* logical, rational. I'm sick and someone we trust, someone who knows all about these things, is telling us they have a cure. Of, but, of sorts, but they don't. They don't. All they have is a solution to a problem we didn't even think we had until they started talking it up. And I'm sorry. I'm sorry. I am so desperately sorry, Carrie. Because I wish I had met, *we* had met, I

wish that we had met years ago. An age ago. It is unfair.
It is so crushingly – And I feel a resentment, a great great
resentment and an anger, an anger, in the pit of my, when
I think about all the years I wasted not knowing you . . .
And about all the years I won't have to get to know you
better . . . But – Look at me, look at me – Because I mean
this – You will *never* –

Carrie I understand I understand . . . I'm sorry, thank
you, but I can't keep talking . . . like this, I'm sorry . . .
I feel sick I feel sick we need to stop talking about it.
I hear you. I hear you. I hear you.

 Beat. The longest one yet, perhaps.

What will we do instead?

Lorna Cope.

ONE

Lorna, Carrie and Miriam.

Miriam The damage, the deterioration, is more advanced –

Lorna Further along?

Miriam Yes.

Lorna Further along than you thought?

Carrie And worse than you thought, too, or –

Miriam It is, yes.

Lorna How?

Miriam The disease doesn't work chronologically, or even logically –

Lorna But the, the spread of it –

Miriam Yes –

Lorna The rate of the spread of it –

Miriam Yes, that's correct, the speed with which –

Lorna Is worse?

Miriam Than we had anticipated, expected, let's say, at this stage, that's correct.

Carrie What can we do?

Miriam Would you like to sit down by the way?

Carrie No. Thank you. Me, you mean?

Miriam Both of you.

Carrie I'm too jittery to – You?

Lorna I'm fine.

Miriam Something to drink?

Lorna Please don't prevaricate.

Miriam When we last spoke, we discussed the possibility of, the specific removal of a series of, very localised, particular networks of neurons, in order to stem the spread of the disease. But that, to speak plainly, is no longer an option. It would appear a slightly more elaborate procedure is now our only – A neural, for instance, a neural prosthesis of some description.

Lorna Prosthetic?

Miriam Yes.

Lorna You mean a synthetic bit of brain?

Miriam A silicon, yes, a silicon chip, to replace or heal any damaged or indeed absent brain tissue, absent neurons, pathways. Using the information from your simulation, we can, are able to, to programme – To cut a long story – A very specific mathematical formula is, can be, programmed into the prosthetic –

Lorna The chip?

Miriam Into the chip, yes, so that there is no loss of function as a result of any tissue we remove.

Lorna Anything you take you can put back in.

Miriam In terms of functionality, yes. But in terms of memories associated with particular pathways or any tissue we have to remove, no. That which we have to remove will be permanently lost to you. As if it were never there in the first place.

Lorna Jesus.

Miriam It's the difference between not being able to remember where you left your house keys, and having your house burnt down.

This seems to sting both Lorna and Carrie a little more than Miriam had intended.

Lorna You mean there'll be no going back, is what you mean, what she means.

Miriam Correct. This is an asymmetrical procedure.

Lorna To be absolutely clear.

Miriam Please.

Lorna The information you have to remove, however much that might end up being, there is no way you can, I don't know, programme that into this, chip, this prosthetic?

Miriam No –

Lorna You can't create a programme for that and return it –

Miriam The memory, no, the brain doesn't – Despite various analogies to the contrary, the brain in no way – We're not machines. Memory, memories, are not data. They aren't stored or filed away. They're non-linear, associative. Reliant on context, bound by time and space, millions of things happening all at once. I say to you coffee and you might say to me: brown. Bitter. But you might also say, a, a name, or a place.

Lorna You haven't answered my question.

Miriam There were, there has been some research into the, yes, into the creation, into hippocampal prosthesis, a prosthetic hippocampus which is programmed to re-create very precise patterns of electrochemical activity associated with particular memories. But only, so far, in mice –

Lorna Mice?

Miriam Yes. And rats. Mice and rats and zebra fish. But, the results weren't particularly . . . encouraging.

Lorna Meaning?

Miriam There was evidence of psychosis, of –

Lorna Psychosis?

Miriam Correct.

Lorna Mouse psychosis?

Miriam Unlikely as it sounds –

Lorna Tiny mice with tiny bouts of –

Miriam I know it must sound, a little, somewhat let's say unreal, but –

Lorna Worse than unreal, it sounds ridiculous!

Carrie Lorna.

Lorna What? It's embarrassing!

Carrie Enough.

Beat.

I'd like to go back. To the procedure we were discussing. For Lorna. The procedure you're recommending. How many times have you carried out this particular procedure? The one you are recommending to us today, right now.

Miriam I've lost count.

Carrie It works, then, you believe, believe that it works?

Miriam The results speak for themselves, yes.

Carrie And what about the times when you've seen it not? Work, fail, go all to shit, on those occasions –

Miriam I have never seen this procedure fail. It is complex, and you know what, it can be arduous, let's be clear about that, particularly during the, recovery. But it works. Time and time and time again. Phobias, obsessive compulsive disorder, post-traumatic stress, addiction – All treatable, all curable.

Carrie Wow.

Lorna But it's a, where do you even begin . . .

Miriam It's a lot, for sure.

Lorna What happens to me? What's going to happen to, what's going to bind me, this me, now, to me once I wake up, and you've . . .

Miriam We're talking about a very small, a very specific, relatively small amount of –

Lorna How small exactly?

Miriam I'm sorry?

Lorna You said small . . . the . . . with . . .

But Lorna has 'gone blank'. Beat.

Sorry, I . . .

Beat.

No, it's gone, I'm sorry. I was . . . No I don't, know what I was . . . I'm sorry.

Carrie You don't need to apologise.

Lorna Still getting used to, going like that, losing my train of . . .

Beat.

Have you ever, any personal experience, with, in this particular, have you ever –

Miriam Meaning the procedure itself, or –

Lorna No, personally. This, all this, the mind running a mile.

Miriam My mother, actually, yes, she –

Lorna Your mother –

Miriam Yes, she –

Lorna What did you do?

Miriam Well. You know what – she died.

Lorna Why?

Miriam 'Why'?

Carrie Lorna –

Lorna Why didn't you intervene?

Miriam She, well, she had made it very clear to us that that was not what she wanted.

Lorna Really?

Miriam doesn't respond.

How old was she?

Miriam I'd rather not . . . She was in her eighties, eighties, eighty-seven.

Lorna She said no?

Miriam She did.

Lorna And what did you do?

Miriam I bore witness to it.

Lorna I'm sorry.

Miriam Yes.

Carrie Is there anything else that we –

Lorna But what would you have done, if she, if she had agreed?

Miriam I'm sorry, I'm somewhat uncomfortable –

Lorna Please. If you don't mind. I would like to know how –

Carrie Enough.

Lorna I'm sorry – I'm really not –

Miriam It's okay, it's okay. It's a very big decision. And I understand the need for information. So here are the facts. My mother died unable to swallow. By and large unable to move. To speak. To call for help. To think. To comprehend her surroundings. To differentiate between time and place and past and present. Unable even to hold my gaze, to clasp my hand. Now you might say, well this is natural, so is life. This is ageing. And twenty, thirty years ago I might have agreed with you. *Might*. But not any more. Ageing is a disease, on this we can agree. It appears natural, so-called, but it need not be. At least when it comes to the mind. The body, yes, the body, it may decay. And it will most certainly die. But the mind, the brain, this three pounds of mass, we now have a way to augment. To treat, to cure, to preserve. To enhance. And before you – No, it isn't about living for ever. It isn't about – But what it is about, is a good death, so-called. Quality of life. And that is my job. There are some, yes, there are those who wish to free the mind from the body. To roam free. I don't know, I don't know about that. I want to help you, Lorna. It would be remiss of me not – I would not be doing my job . . . You know what, no, I don't know what else I can say to you.

57

Beat.

Carrie If we wait?

Miriam I'm sorry?

Carrie To come to a decision, what are the consequences of waiting.

Miriam The disease is progressive. The longer, if you – It's degenerative, it's . . .

Lorna I can't help but think I'm with your mother on this one. It's abhorrent. Isn't it, this, all this.

Carrie Or –

Lorna Isn't it?

Carrie Or it's a –

Lorna Isn't it, all this, it's –

Carrie Or it's a, or it might be the opposite. It could be right. Because you'll be better. And that is, you know, surely, that is – Yeah I mean as far as I'm concerned, that is, the single most important – And so yeah whatever it takes to, to get to that, to get to that point, whatever it . . .

Lorna is silent.

(*To Miriam.*) I think we ought to, think we're going to need to, take some, before we –

Miriam Of course.

Carrie But thank you. It's all very – The need, the need for expediency, I think it's, I think we, don't we? Clear, you've made it – And we will, won't we, come to a . . . (*To Lorna.*) Won't we? Together.

Living Through Change

'I can only note that the past is beautiful because one never realises an emotion at the time. It expands later, and thus we don't have complete emotions about the present, only about the past.'

Virginia Woolf

Loss of memory evokes a particular quality of fear, both for the person whose memory is fading and those close to them. Throughout her career, Deborah Bowman, Professor of Bioethics, Clinical Ethics and Medical Law, has worked with numerous individuals, families and clinicians navigating the painful and frightening prospect of dementia and memory loss. Here she shares her experience and how the law informs such highly emotive situations.

As human beings, we navigate denial of our mortality and dread of illness throughout our lives. Within families, we have our own pathographies which cause us to dread specific diseases and fates. Yet, diseases that affect our capacity and memory prompt a unique type of apprehension. For what are we without our memories? Perhaps more significantly, *who* are we when our memories are compromised, diminished or lost?

These are questions that many are facing. In 2015, there were estimated to be over 850,000 people living with dementia. The Alzheimer's Society predicts that if current trends continue, over a million people in the UK will have dementia by 2025 and over two million by 2051. Globally, it is thought that over 36 million people are affected by dementia and, of those, approximately 28 million are undiagnosed.

Diseases that affect memory alter identities. The plural noun is important. For memories are embedded within our relationships, roles and communities. What we remember reflects who we are to other people. Our stories are informed by, and inform, the stories of others. We depend on each other as we develop our identities: as someone's child, sibling, friend, lover, partner or colleague. And we, in turn, hold up the mirror of identity to those whose lives entwine with our own.

The effects of a loss of memory on identity can be devastating both for the one affected and for those who love and know that person. Often it is the small, but searing, reminders that someone has been altered by disease that are the most painful. Moments that represent much more. A woman who, on arriving at a care home, was heartbroken to see her *Guardian* newspaper reading friend randomly turning the pages of the *Sun* described the overwhelming sadness she felt at the sight. Children of a lifelong vegetarian who found their mother tucking in to sausages on a hospital ward grappled with whether they should ask staff to withhold meat in recognition of their mother's long-held principles, or simply be grateful her food seemed to give her pleasure. The cumulative effect of these moment-by-moment changes remind us what is lost: a person's identity and the landscape of our relationship are, we realise, irrevocably altered.

However, it is seductively appealing to misrepresent the coherence of memory and to suggest there is a clear boundary between those whose memories are compromised by illness and those who enjoy 'healthy' memories. For memory is a slippery and mysterious phenomenon. We appear in photographs that prove our presence at events we don't recall. We filter, sift, enhance, disregard, deny and emphasise moments in our lives to create a narrative that we package and repackage according to context and time. We are floored by the rush of unanticipated recollection on hearing a piece of music or smelling something that reminds us of times and people about which we have not thought for years. We wake shaken from vivid dreams that cast us back during sleep into a muddled mosaic of people, periods and places often overlaid with chaotic surrealism. With friends and family, we negotiate and argue about our experiences: who was there, what were we wearing, was the weather really apocalyptic? We sort through the memories that each person offers to achieve a shared account. And, of course, the process of building the common story from the pieces of individual recollections is, itself, identity-forming and memory-creating.

Even if we had the capacity to remember our lives and experiences accurately and completely, would we wish to do so anyway? The question of constancy and change is especially interesting in thinking about what we do and do not remember. Human beings change: physically, emotionally, politically and socially. Some of those changes are chosen and pursued, some are mediated by relationships, psychological development and social shifts, some come about by luck or ill-fortune. Nonetheless, change is a feature of our identities and our lives. Paradoxically, constancy, particularly in relationships, is often possible because we acknowledge and allow for change in ourselves and in others.

It is in this complex and shifting context that decisions about healthcare take place. Loss of memory does not necessarily mean loss of capacity. Capacity is a legal concept that depends on what someone can understand, retain and consider to make a choice. It is dynamic and is decision-specific. It depends on function, not diagnosis.

Nonetheless, and sadly, many diseases do impair one's capacity, thereby reducing or removing an individual's autonomy. The challenge for clinicians is to work with families towards caring and practical solutions.

There are several ways in which we can plan for a diminution in, or loss of, capacity and the law presents a number of options. Some people make advance decisions: statements of preference or choice about a future event and time. Advance decisions are not without challenges. First, they are predicated on the notion that we can know our future selves and predict wishes in relation to symptoms we have not yet experienced. Secondly, advance decisions have to be sufficiently clear and precise as to apply to a specific set of circumstances – a requirement that depends on an honest and informed appraisal of the development of an illness.

Another option is for an individual anticipating the loss of capacity to nominate someone to act as a proxy and to make choices on his or her behalf: a lasting power of attorney. Usually, the power of attorney is held by someone who knows the individual well. The holder of a power of attorney must act in the patient's best interests. It is a legal relationship, but it is often founded on love; and therein lies its power and its limitations. Love may create a strong advocate who will ensure that care reflects what an individual would have chosen. However, love may also mean that the person holding the power of attorney feels overwhelmed and conflicted by their responsibilities at an already painful time.

The emotional impact, and even the burden, of making significant healthcare decisions for another person can be considerable. The law provides a framework within which to operate, but even when there have been searching discussions about someone's preferences regarding care, suffering, dignity and death, the gap between agreement in the abstract, and the reality of determining what happens to someone you love can be vast and over-whelming. If the person holding the lasting power of attorney is also the patient's lover, sibling, child or spouse, he or she is steering a course through their own sense of loss and grief at the damage that illness has wrought.

What then might the ethical response be to someone who has impaired or lost memory? It is, I suggest, to do something that is simultaneously simple and difficult: to accept the person as he or she is now with compassion, empathy and acceptance. No matter how developed medical science becomes or how thoroughly we develop our understanding of disease, to attend to another person as he or she *is*, not as one would *wish* them to be, will always be a transformative act of care.

DEBORAH BOWMAN

Deborah Bowman is Professor of Bioethics, Clinical Ethics and Medical Law as well as Dean of Students at St George's, University of London, and Editor-in-Chief at Medical Humanities Journal

mh.bmj.com   @deborahbowman

The Science of Selfhood

> The brain is wider than the sky,
> For, put them side by side,
> The one the other would contain,
> With ease, and you besides.

> Emily Dickinson,
> *Complete Poems*, 1924

What does it mean to be a self? And what happens to the social fabric of life, to our ethics and morality, when the nature of selfhood is called into question?

In neuroscience and psychology, the experience of 'being a self' has long been a central concern. One of the most important lessons, from decades of research, is that there is no single thing that is the self. Rather, the self is better thought of as an integrated network of processes that distinguish self from non-self at many different levels. There is the bodily self – the experience of identifying with and owning a particular body, which at a more fundamental level involves the amorphous experience of *being* a self-sustaining organism. There is the perspectival self, the experience of perceiving the world from a particular first-person point-of-view. The volitional self involves experiences of intention, of agency, of urges to do this or that (or, perhaps more importantly, to refrain from doing this or that) and of being the cause of things that happen.

At higher levels we encounter narrative and social selves. The narrative self is where the 'I' comes in, as the experience of being a continuous and distinctive person over time. This narrative self – the story we tell ourselves

about who we are – is built from a rich set of autobiographical memories that are associated with a particular
subject. Finally, the social self is that aspect of my self-
experience and personal identity that depends on my
social milieu, on how others perceive and behave towards
me, and on how I perceive myself through their eyes and
minds.

In daily life, it can be hard to differentiate these dimensions
of selfhood. We move through the world as seemingly
unified wholes, our experience of bodily self seamlessly
integrated with our memories from the past, and with
our experiences of volition and agency. But introspection
can be a poor guide. Many experiments and neuropsycho-
logical case studies tell a rather different story, one in
which the brain actively and continuously generates and
coordinates these diverse aspects of self-experience.

The many ways of being a self can come apart in
surprising and revealing situations. For example, it is
remarkably easy to alter the experience of bodily selfhood.
In the so-called 'rubber-hand illusion', I ask you to focus
your attention on a fake hand while your real hand is
kept out of sight. If I then simultaneously stroke your real
hand and the fake hand with a soft paintbrush, you may
develop the uncanny feeling that the fake hand is now,
somehow, part of your body. A more dramatic disturbance
of the experience of body ownership happens in somato-
paraphrenia, a condition in which people experience that
part of their body as no longer theirs, that it belongs to
someone else – perhaps their doctor or family member.
Both these examples involve changes in brain activity, in
particular within the 'temporo-parietal junction',
showing how even very basic aspects of personal identity
are actively constructed by the brain.

Moving through levels of selfhood, autoscopic hallucinations involve seeing oneself from a different perspective,

66

much like in 'out of body' experiences. In akinetic mutism, people seem to lack any experiences of volition or intention (and do very little), while in schizophrenia or anarchic hand syndrome, people can experience their intentions or voluntary actions as having external causes. At the other end of the spectrum, disturbances of social self emerge in autism, where difficulties in perceiving others' states of mind seems to be a core problem, though the exact nature of the autistic condition is still much debated.

When it comes to the 'I', memory is the key. Specifically, autobiographical memory: the recollection of personal experiences of people, objects, places and other episodes from an individual's life. While there are as many types of memory as there are varieties of self (for example, we have separate memory processes for facts, for the short term and the long term, and for skills that we learn), autobiographical memories are those most closely associated with our sense of personal identity. This is well illustrated by some classic medical cases in which, as a result of surgery or disease, the ability to lay down new memories is lost. In 1953 Henry Molaison (also known as the patient HM) had large parts of his medial temporal lobes removed in order to relieve severe epilepsy. From 1957 until his death in 2008, HM was studied closely by the neuropsychologist Brenda Milner, yet he was never able to remember meeting her. In 1985 the accomplished musician Clive Wearing suffered a severe viral brain disease that affected similar parts of his brain. Now seventy-seven, he frequently believes he has just awoken from a coma, spending each day in a constant state of re-awakening.

Surprisingly, both HM and Wearing remained able to learn new skills, forming new 'procedural' memories, despite never recalling the learning process itself. Wearing could still play the piano, and conduct his choir, though he would immediately forget having done so. The music appears to carry him along from moment to moment, restoring his sense of self in a way his memory no longer can. And his love for his wife Deborah seems undiminished, so that he expresses an enormous sense of joy on seeing her, even though he cannot tell whether their last meeting was years, or seconds, in the past. Love, it seems, persists when much else is gone.

For people like HM and Clive Wearing, memory loss has been unintended and unwanted. But as scientific understanding develops, could we be moving towards a world where specific memories and elements of our identity can be isolated or removed through medical intervention? And could the ability to lay down new memories ever be surgically restored? Some recent breakthroughs suggest these developments may not be all that far-fetched.

In 2013, Jason Chan and Jessica LaPaglia, from Iowa State University, showed that specific human memories could indeed be deleted. They took advantage of the fact that when memories are explicitly recalled they become more vulnerable. By changing details about a memory, while it was being remembered, they induced a selective amnesia which lasted for at least twenty-four hours. Although an important advance, this experiment was limited by relying on 'non-invasive' methods – not using drugs or directly interfering with the brain.

More recent animal experiments have shown even more striking effects. In a ground-breaking 2014 study at the University of California, using genetically engineered mice, Sadegh Nabavi and colleagues managed to block and then reactivate a specific memory. They used a powerful (invasive) technique called optogenetics to activate (or inactivate) the biochemical processes determining how neurons change their connectivity. And

68

elsewhere in California, Ted Berger is working on the first prototypes of so-called 'hippocampal prostheses' which replace a part of the brain essential for memory with a computer chip. Although these advances are still a long way from implementation in humans, they show an extraordinary potential for future medical interventions.

The German philosopher Thomas Metzinger believes that 'no such things as selves exist in the world'. Modern neuroscience may be on his side, with memory being only one thread in the rich tapestry of processes shaping our sense of selfhood. At the same time, the world outside the laboratory is still full of people who experience themselves – and each other – as distinct, integrated wholes. How the new science of selfhood will change this everyday lived experience, and society with it, is a story that is yet to be told.

ANIL K. SETH

Anil K. Smith is Professor of Cognitive and Computational Neuroscience, and Co-Director of the Sackler Centre for Consciousness Science, University of Sussex

www.anilseth.com   @anilkseth

FURTHER READING

A. K. Seth, ed., *Thirty Second Brain* (Ivy Press, 2014)
T. Metzinger, *The Ego Tunnel* (Basic Books, 2009)
D. Wearing, *Forever Today: A Memoir of Love and Amnesia* (Corgi, 2005)